MAD LIBS®
MEOW LIBS

by Sarah Fabiny

MAD LIBS
An Imprint of Penguin Random House LLC, New York

Photo credit: cover, page 1: (American Polydactyl kitten sitting, looking at the camera)
© Thinkstock, photo by GlobalP

Mad Libs format and text copyright © 2015 by Penguin Random House LLC.
All rights reserved.

Concept created by Roger Price & Leonard Stern

Published by Mad Libs,
an imprint of Penguin Random House LLC, New York.
Printed in the USA.

Visit us online at www.penguinrandomhouse.com.

ISBN 9780843182927
29

MAD LIBS is a registered trademark of Penguin Random House LLC.

INSTRUCTIONS

MAD LIBS® is a game for people who don't like games! It can be played by one, two, three, four, or forty.

● RIDICULOUSLY SIMPLE DIRECTIONS

In this tablet you will find stories containing blank spaces where words are left out. One player, the READER, selects one of these stories. The READER does not tell anyone what the story is about. Instead, he/she asks the other players, the WRITERS, to give him/her words. These words are used to fill in the blank spaces in the story.

● TO PLAY

The READER asks each WRITER in turn to call out a word—an adjective or a noun or whatever the space calls for—and uses them to fill in the blank spaces in the story. The result is a MAD LIBS® game.

When the READER then reads the completed MAD LIBS® game to the other players, they will discover that they have written a story that is fantastic, screamingly funny, shocking, silly, crazy, or just plain dumb—depending upon which words each WRITER called out.

● EXAMPLE (*Before* and *After*)

"_____!" he said _____
　　　　　EXCLAMATION　　　　　　　　　　　　　　　　ADVERB

as he jumped into his convertible _____ and
　　　　　　　　　　　　　　　　　　　　　　NOUN

drove off with his _____ wife.
　　　　　　　　　　ADJECTIVE

"_____*Ouch*_____!" he said _____*stupidly*_____
　　　　　EXCLAMATION　　　　　　　　　　　　　　　　ADVERB

as he jumped into his convertible _____*cat*_____ and
　　　　　　　　　　　　　　　　　　　　　　NOUN

drove off with his _____*brave*_____ wife.
　　　　　　　　　　ADJECTIVE

In case you have forgotten what adjectives, adverbs, nouns, and verbs are, here is a quick review:

An ADJECTIVE describes something or somebody. *Lumpy*, *soft*, *ugly*, *messy*, and *short* are adjectives.

An ADVERB tells how something is done. It modifies a verb and usually ends in "ly." *Modestly*, *stupidly*, *greedily*, and *carefully* are adverbs.

A NOUN is the name of a person, place, or thing. *Sidewalk*, *umbrella*, *bridle*, *bathtub*, and *nose* are nouns.

A VERB is an action word. *Run*, *pitch*, *jump*, and *swim* are verbs. Put the verbs in past tense if the directions say PAST TENSE. *Ran*, *pitched*, *jumped*, and *swam* are verbs in the past tense.

When we ask for A PLACE, we mean any sort of place: a country or city (*Spain*, *Cleveland*) or a room (*bathroom*, *kitchen*).

An EXCLAMATION or SILLY WORD is any sort of funny sound, gasp, grunt, or outcry, like *Wow!*, *Ouch!*, *Whomp!*, *Ick!*, and *Gadzooks!*

When we ask for specific words, like a NUMBER, a COLOR, an ANIMAL, or a PART OF THE BODY, we mean a word that is one of those things, like *seven*, *blue*, *horse*, or *head*.

When we ask for a PLURAL, it means more than one. For example, *cat* pluralized is *cats*.

MAD LIBS® is fun to play with friends, but you can also play it by yourself! To begin with, DO NOT look at the story on the page below. Fill in the blanks on this page with the words called for. Then, using the words you have selected, fill in the blank spaces in the story.

Now you've created your own hilarious MAD LIBS® game!

FAMOUS CATS

ADJECTIVE _____

NOUN _____

NUMBER _____

TYPE OF FOOD _____

PLURAL NOUN _____

VERB _____

PERSON IN ROOM _____

PERSON IN ROOM (FEMALE) _____

PLURAL NOUN _____

NOUN _____

PART OF THE BODY _____

A PLACE _____

PERSON IN ROOM (FEMALE) _____

ADJECTIVE _____

ANIMAL _____

MAD LIBS®

FAMOUS CATS

From cartoons to social media, cats are everywhere. Here are a few of

the most famous cats:

- Morris—the cat with the _____ attitude and the posh
  ADJECTIVE

  _____ is the "spokesperson" for _____ Lives cat
  NOUN   NUMBER

  _____.
  TYPE OF FOOD

- Garfield—the famous comic-strip cat who hates _____,
  PLURAL NOUN

  loves to _____, and has no respect for _____,
  VERB   PERSON IN ROOM

  his owner's dog.

- Smelly Cat—made famous in the song sung by

  _____ on the TV show _____.
  PERSON IN ROOM (FEMALE)   PLURAL NOUN

- Grumpy Cat—an Internet _____ known for her hilarious
  NOUN

  _____ expressions.
  PART OF THE BODY

- Stubbs—the mayor of (the) _____, Alaska.
  A PLACE

- Cat—the feline heroine of the movie *Breakfast at*

  _____'s.
  PERSON IN ROOM (FEMALE)

- Tom—the _____ cat that will never catch his archenemy,
  ADJECTIVE

  Jerry the _____.
  ANIMAL

MAD LIBS® is fun to play with friends, but you can also play it by yourself! To begin with, DO NOT look at the story on the page below. Fill in the blanks on this page with the words called for. Then, using the words you have selected, fill in the blank spaces in the story.

Now you've created your own hilarious MAD LIBS® game!

WHICH BREED IS RIGHT FOR YOU?

PART OF THE BODY (PLURAL) _____

ADJECTIVE _____

NOUN _____

ADJECTIVE _____

NOUN _____

NOUN _____

PART OF THE BODY (PLURAL) _____

ADJECTIVE _____

NOUN _____

SILLY WORD _____

ADJECTIVE _____

A PLACE _____

ADJECTIVE _____

PART OF THE BODY _____

COLOR _____

ADJECTIVE _____

NOUN _____

So you're thinking of getting a cat. Whether you prefer cats with

no _____ or _____ ears, there's a/an
    PART OF THE BODY (PLURAL)   ADJECTIVE

_____ for you.
    NOUN

Sphynx: If you go for the _____ things in life, and don't want
                           ADJECTIVE

to have to clean up cat hair, this is the _____ for you.
                                  NOUN

Siamese: Do you want a cat that sounds like a crying _____ and
                                       NOUN

has crossed _____? Well then, go get a Siamese.
          PART OF THE BODY (PLURAL)

Manx: Looking for a cat with a sweet, _____ face and no
                           ADJECTIVE

_____? We suggest you get a/an _____.
  NOUN   SILLY WORD

Maine coon: How about a cat that's the size of a/an _____
                                         ADJECTIVE

dog? If you don't mind having to brush your cat every day, it sounds

like you should get a/an _____ coon.
                       A PLACE

Persian: If you love a/an _____-looking cat with a scrunched-
                          ADJECTIVE

up _____, go get yourself a Persian.
    PART OF THE BODY

Snowshoe: Do you love a cat with adorable _____ feet and a/an
                                     COLOR

_____ personality? You may want a/an _____-shoe.
  ADJECTIVE   NOUN

MAD LIBS® is fun to play with friends, but you can also play it by yourself! To begin with, DO NOT look at the story on the page below. Fill in the blanks on this page with the words called for. Then, using the words you have selected, fill in the blank spaces in the story.

Now you've created your own hilarious MAD LIBS® game!

CAT SAYINGS

ADJECTIVE _____

PLURAL NOUN _____

PART OF THE BODY _____

NOUN _____

SILLY WORD _____

ADJECTIVE _____

VERB ENDING IN "ING" _____

ARTICLE OF CLOTHING _____

ADJECTIVE _____

NOUN _____

ANIMAL _____

NOUN _____

NOUN _____

EXCLAMATION _____

ADJECTIVE _____

ADVERB _____

ADJECTIVE _____

MAD LIBS®
CAT SAYINGS

There are a lot of _____ phrases that incorporate our favorite
             ADJECTIVE

feline _____. Check out these sayings and their meanings:
    PLURAL NOUN

- Cat got your _____?: Why aren't you talking?
           PART OF THE BODY

- You let the cat out of the _____: _____! My secret
             NOUN   SILLY WORD

  isn't so _____ anymore.
     ADJECTIVE

- It is raining cats and dogs: It is _____ like crazy.
        VERB ENDING IN "ING"

- That is the cat's _____: That is totally _____!
     ARTICLE OF CLOTHING   ADJECTIVE

- When the cat's away, the mice will play: The boss is away—let's get

  this _____ started!
   NOUN

- Curiosity killed the _____: Mind your own _____!
        ANIMAL   NOUN

- He is a fat cat: He likes to flash his _____.
        NOUN

- Looks like something the cat dragged in: _____! You look
        EXCLAMATION

  _____. What happened?!
  ADJECTIVE

- Cat on a hot tin roof: Please sit _____!
      ADVERB

- It's like herding cats: This job is totally _____!
        ADJECTIVE

MAD LIBS® is fun to play with friends, but you can also play it by yourself! To begin with, DO NOT look at the story on the page below. Fill in the blanks on this page with the words called for. Then, using the words you have selected, fill in the blank spaces in the story.

Now you've created your own hilarious MAD LIBS® game!

CAT SHOWS

ADJECTIVE _____

ADJECTIVE _____

ADJECTIVE _____

VERB _____

NOUN _____

SAME NOUN _____

NOUN _____

NOUN _____

PLURAL NOUN _____

PLURAL NOUN _____

NOUN _____

A PLACE _____

PLURAL NOUN _____

ADJECTIVE _____

NOUN _____

MAD LIBS

CAT SHOWS

There are some cat owners who take their love of cats to a/an

_____ level. A/An _____ example of this: the
  ADJECTIVE   ADJECTIVE

cat show. Both _____ and purebred cats are allowed
                     ADJECTIVE

to _____ in a cat show, although the rules differ from
       VERB

_____ to _____. The cats are compared to a breed
     NOUN   SAME NOUN

_____, and those judged to be closest to it are awarded
     NOUN

a/an _____. At the end of the year, all the _____
          NOUN   PLURAL NOUN

who won at various shows are tallied up, and regional and national

_____ are presented. The very first cat _____ took
  PLURAL NOUN   NOUN

place in 1598 at (the) _____ in England. In the United States,
                          A PLACE

the first cat shows were held at New England country _____
                                                          PLURAL NOUN

in the 1860s. The most important cat show in the United States is the

CFA _____ Cat Show. But no matter which cat wins "Best
        ADJECTIVE

in Show," every cat is a/an _____—to their owners, at least!
                                  NOUN

MAD LIBS® is fun to play with friends, but you can also play it by yourself! To begin with, DO NOT look at the story on the page below. Fill in the blanks on this page with the words called for. Then, using the words you have selected, fill in the blank spaces in the story.

Now you've created your own hilarious MAD LIBS® game!

CATS IN THE NEWS

PLURAL NOUN _____

ADJECTIVE _____

NOUN _____

ADJECTIVE _____

NUMBER _____

NOUN _____

NOUN _____

NOUN _____

SAME NOUN _____

ADJECTIVE _____

NOUN _____

ADJECTIVE _____

NOUN _____

VERB _____

MAD LIBS

CATS IN THE NEWS

News Anchor #1: Stay tuned, _____! After the commercial
<u>PLURAL NOUN</u>

break, we have a/an _____ story about a cat who saved a
<u>ADJECTIVE</u>

young _____ from a/an _____ dog.
<u>NOUN</u>   <u>ADJECTIVE</u>

News Anchor #2: That reminds me of the story about the cat that

dialed _____-1-1 after its owner fell out of his _____.
<u>NUMBER</u>   <u>NOUN</u>

News Anchor #1: And how about that kitten that survived the deadly

_____ in Taiwan?
<u>NOUN</u>

News Anchor #2: Have you heard about the kitten that was saved

from a/an _____ by a/an _____-fighter with
<u>NOUN</u>   <u>SAME NOUN</u>

_____ water and a/an _____ full of oxygen?
<u>ADJECTIVE</u>   <u>NOUN</u>

News Anchor #1: And who could forget that _____ story
<u>ADJECTIVE</u>

about a cat that took a/an _____ on the London Underground?
<u>NOUN</u>

News Anchor #2: Well, I guess he had to _____ to work just
<u>VERB</u>

like everyone else!

MAD LIBS® is fun to play with friends, but you can also play it by yourself! To begin with, DO NOT look at the story on the page below. Fill in the blanks on this page with the words called for. Then, using the words you have selected, fill in the blank spaces in the story.

Now you've created your own hilarious MAD LIBS® game!

HISTORY OF CATS

VERB ENDING IN "ING" _____

NUMBER _____

ADJECTIVE _____

ANIMAL (PLURAL) _____

SAME ANIMAL (PLURAL) _____

ADJECTIVE _____

PLURAL NOUN _____

ADJECTIVE _____

PART OF THE BODY _____

ADJECTIVE _____

OCCUPATION (PLURAL) _____

VERB (PAST TENSE) _____

ADJECTIVE _____

ADJECTIVE _____

NUMBER _____

ADJECTIVE _____

MAD LIBS

HISTORY OF CATS

Cats have been _____ with—or at least tolerating—
_____VERB ENDING IN "ING"_____

people for over _____ years. Cats first became a part of
_____NUMBER_____

our _____ lives when people started to grow grain. The
_____ADJECTIVE_____

grain attracted _____, and the cats preyed on the
_____ANIMAL (PLURAL)_____

_____. Cats soon became a/an _____
_____SAME ANIMAL (PLURAL)_____   _____ADJECTIVE_____

fixture in peoples' _____ and were even worshipped in
_____PLURAL NOUN_____

_____ Egypt. There was even an Egyptian goddess that had
_____ADJECTIVE_____

the _____ of a cat! However, in the _____ Ages,
_____PART OF THE BODY_____   _____ADJECTIVE_____

cats came to be demonized and were thought to be affiliated with evil

_____. Many cats were _____ to ward off evil.
_____OCCUPATION (PLURAL)_____   _____VERB (PAST TENSE)_____

In the 1600s, the cat's _____ reputation was restored, and
_____ADJECTIVE_____

today cats are _____ stars and live in _____ percent
_____ADJECTIVE_____   _____NUMBER_____

of American households. Talk about a long and _____ history!
_____ADJECTIVE_____

MAD LIBS® is fun to play with friends, but you can also play it by yourself! To begin with, DO NOT look at the story on the page below. Fill in the blanks on this page with the words called for. Then, using the words you have selected, fill in the blank spaces in the story.

Now you've created your own hilarious MAD LIBS® game!

I AM A CAT LADY

ADJECTIVE _____

ADJECTIVE _____

PLURAL NOUN _____

NUMBER _____

ADJECTIVE _____

ADJECTIVE _____

VERB _____

ADJECTIVE _____

PLURAL NOUN _____

ADVERB _____

ADVERB _____

NOUN _____

ADJECTIVE _____

ADJECTIVE _____

ADJECTIVE _____

ANIMAL _____

MAD LIBS

I AM A CAT LADY

Dear _____ Neighbor,
      ADJECTIVE

I'm glad we have come to a/an _____ understanding about our
                        ADJECTIVE

_____. You have come to accept my _____ cats, and I
PLURAL NOUN   NUMBER

have come to accept your _____ dog. Yes, my _____
                   ADJECTIVE   ADJECTIVE

cats may _____ in your garden, but your _____
        VERB   ADJECTIVE

dog digs up my _____. And I will remind you that my cats
          PLURAL NOUN

purr very _____, while your dog barks _____. To
        ADVERB   ADVERB

conclude, I feel sorry for the _____-man, who is scared of
                         NOUN

your _____ dog, while he brings treats for my _____
    ADJECTIVE   ADJECTIVE

felines. I'm glad we have been able to come to a/an _____
                                   ADJECTIVE

understanding on this matter.

Yours truly,

The _____ Lady Next Door
    ANIMAL

MAD LIBS® is fun to play with friends, but you can also play it by yourself! To begin with, DO NOT look at the story on the page below. Fill in the blanks on this page with the words called for. Then, using the words you have selected, fill in the blank spaces in the story.

Now you've created your own hilarious MAD LIBS® game!

CATS ON CAMERA

ADJECTIVE _____

VERB ENDING IN "ING" _____

NOUN _____

SILLY WORD _____

ADJECTIVE _____

ADJECTIVE _____

NOUN _____

NOUN _____

NOUN _____

EXCLAMATION _____

VERB ENDING IN "S" _____

NOUN _____

ADJECTIVE _____

NUMBER _____

ADJECTIVE _____

PLURAL NOUN _____

MAD LIBS®

CATS ON CAMERA

Cat Lover #1: Have you seen the _____ video on YouTube of
ADJECTIVE

the cat _____ a/an _____?
VERB ENDING IN "ING" _NOUN_

Cat Lover #2: _____! It's almost as _____ as that
SILLY WORD _ADJECTIVE_

GIF of the _____ kitten playing with a/an _____.
ADJECTIVE _NOUN_

Cat Lover #1: And that clip of the _____ cat who pushes her
NOUN

own _____ down some stairs?! _____!
NOUN _EXCLAMATION_

Cat Lover #2: How about the cat who _____ along to
VERB ENDING IN "S"

a/an _____ video? Totally _____!
NOUN _ADJECTIVE_

Cat Lover #1: And there must be about _____ videos of
NUMBER

_____ cats that have gotten stuck in _____.
ADJECTIVE _PLURAL NOUN_

Cat Lover #2: Yep! And I think I've watched them all.

MAD LIBS® is fun to play with friends, but you can also play it by yourself! To begin with, DO NOT look at the story on the page below. Fill in the blanks on this page with the words called for. Then, using the words you have selected, fill in the blank spaces in the story.

Now you've created your own hilarious MAD LIBS® game!

SEVEN SIGNS YOUR CAT LOVES YOU

ADJECTIVE _____

NOUN _____

SAME NOUN _____

PLURAL NOUN _____

ADJECTIVE _____

VERB _____

NOUN _____

SAME NOUN _____

ADVERB _____

NOUN _____

ADJECTIVE _____

ANIMAL _____

A PLACE _____

ADJECTIVE _____

MAD LIBS
SEVEN SIGNS YOUR CAT LOVES YOU

Here are seven _____ signs your cat loves you:
    _{ADJECTIVE}

• Head butting—If your boyfriend or _____ did this to you,
                                               NOUN

you probably wouldn't want them as your _____ anymore.
                                             SAME NOUN

But when your cat does it, they are marking you with their facial

_____, which shows your cat trusts you.
  PLURAL NOUN

• Powerful purrs—Cats purr for all kinds of reasons, but that

_____ body rumble is saved for expressing true love.
  ADJECTIVE

• Love bites—If your cat likes to _____ on you, it means
                                  VERB

they have a serious _____ for you.
                  NOUN

• Tail twitching—When the tip of a cat's _____ is twitching,
                                      SAME NOUN

it means they are in total control.

• Tummy up—If your cat rolls around on the ground with its tummy

showing, it means they trust you _____.
                               ADVERB

• Kneading—No, your cat doesn't think you are _____
                                        NOUN

dough; he is reliving his _____ memories of kitten hood.
                            ADJECTIVE

• Gifts—You may not want to find a dead _____ in your
                                        ANIMAL

_____, but this is a/an _____ sign of friendship.
  A PLACE   ADJECTIVE

MAD LIBS® is fun to play with friends, but you can also play it by yourself! To begin with, DO NOT look at the story on the page below. Fill in the blanks on this page with the words called for. Then, using the words you have selected, fill in the blank spaces in the story.

Now you've created your own hilarious MAD LIBS® game!

SEVEN SIGNS YOUR CAT IS TRYING TO KILL YOU

ADJECTIVE _____

PLURAL NOUN _____

ADVERB _____

NOUN _____

PART OF THE BODY _____

VERB ENDING IN "ING" _____

ADJECTIVE _____

PART OF THE BODY _____

SILLY WORD _____

NOUN _____

ADVERB _____

ANIMAL _____

ADJECTIVE _____

MAD LIBS
SEVEN SIGNS YOUR CAT IS TRYING TO KILL YOU

There's a flipside to all those _____ expressions of love.
ADJECTIVE

- Head butting—Beware! Your cat is not showing you that it trusts
  you; it's telling you that your _____ are numbered!
  PLURAL NOUN

- Powerful purrs—This is not a sign of true love; it's _____
  ADVERB
  a battle cry!

- Love bites—Not actually a/an _____ of love, but your cat
  NOUN
  tasting you to decide which bit of you to eat first. _____,
  PART OF THE BODY
  please!

- Tail twitching—The equivalent of your cat _____ a
  VERB ENDING IN "ING"
  sword at you.

- Tummy up—Do not fall for this _____ trick! As soon as
  ADJECTIVE
  you put your _____ near your cat's belly, it will scratch
  PART OF THE BODY
  the _____ out of it!
  SILLY WORD

- Kneading—This is not a/an _____ of affection; your cat is
  NOUN
  _____ checking your organs for weaknesses.
  ADVERB

- Gifts—A dead _____ is not a gift; it's a/an _____
  ANIMAL   ADJECTIVE
  warning. Didn't you see *The Godfather*?!

MAD LIBS® is fun to play with friends, but you can also play it by yourself! To begin with, DO NOT look at the story on the page below. Fill in the blanks on this page with the words called for. Then, using the words you have selected, fill in the blank spaces in the story.

Now you've created your own hilarious MAD LIBS® game!

DOGS VERSUS CATS

ADJECTIVE _____

NOUN _____

ADJECTIVE _____

ADJECTIVE _____

ADJECTIVE _____

PART OF THE BODY (PLURAL) _____

NOUN _____

VERB ENDING IN "ING" _____

NOUN _____

ANIMAL _____

NOUN _____

NOUN _____

ADJECTIVE _____

ADVERB _____

ADJECTIVE _____

MAD☺LIBS®

DOGS VERSUS CATS

If you've ever owned both dogs and cats, you know that the differences

between the two species are _____. They are like night and
                              ADJECTIVE

_____. The argument about which pet is more _____
     NOUN   ADJECTIVE

will continue until the end of time, but it's easy to see why cats are

_____. For instance, cats won't embarrass you in front of
  ADJECTIVE

your guests by parading around with your _____ underwear
                                              ADJECTIVE

in their _____. Cats are also funnier than dogs, even
         PART OF THE BODY (PLURAL)

if they don't know it. And they don't give a/an _____ if you
                                                     NOUN

laugh at them, because they are too busy _____ their
                                          VERB ENDING IN "ING"

revenge. Cats are natural _____ repellents—no spider, fly, or
                              NOUN

_____ stands a chance if there's a cat in the _____.
   ANIMAL   NOUN

Cats have no interest in being hooked up to a/an _____ and
                                                     NOUN

going for a walk; they'd rather curl up and take a/an _____
                                                          ADJECTIVE

nap. And it's _____ proven that cat owners are smarter and
                 ADVERB

more _____ than dog owners. So go get yourself a cat!
        ADJECTIVE

MAD LIBS® is fun to play with friends, but you can also play it by yourself! To begin with, DO NOT look at the story on the page below. Fill in the blanks on this page with the words called for. Then, using the words you have selected, fill in the blank spaces in the story.

Now you've created your own hilarious MAD LIBS® game!

MY HOUSE. MY RULES.

ADJECTIVE _____

NOUN _____

VERB _____

NOUN _____

SAME NOUN _____

TYPE OF LIQUID _____

VERB ENDING IN "ING" _____

PERSON IN ROOM (FEMALE) _____

VERB _____

SAME VERB _____

ADJECTIVE _____

ADJECTIVE _____

MAD LIBS

MY HOUSE. MY RULES.

_____ Servant,
ADJECTIVE

It's quite obvious that you think you control me, but we all know that

I am in charge of this _____. You think I am just a simple cat,
NOUN

but I am able to out- _____ you any day of the week. Please be
VERB

aware that "your" house is actually mine, and I am not to be disturbed if

I happen to be sleeping on your bed or favorite piece of _____.
NOUN

I will scratch any piece of _____ I want. I do not want to drink
SAME NOUN

_____ from an ordinary bowl; I prefer to lap water from a/an
TYPE OF LIQUID

_____ faucet or a toilet. So please remember to leave the
VERB ENDING IN "ING"

toilet seat up—I don't care what _____ has to say
PERSON IN ROOM (FEMALE)

about that. Don't try to get me to _____ during the day; you
VERB

should know better than that. I prefer to _____ at night when
SAME VERB

you are asleep; this is much more fun. You are a/an _____
ADJECTIVE

human, but you are my human.

With tolerance,

Your Super- _____ Cat
ADJECTIVE

MAD LIBS® is fun to play with friends, but you can also play it by yourself! To begin with, DO NOT look at the story on the page below. Fill in the blanks on this page with the words called for. Then, using the words you have selected, fill in the blank spaces in the story.

Now you've created your own hilarious MAD LIBS® game!

AM I IN YOUR WAY?

EXCLAMATION _____

NOUN _____

NOUN _____

ADJECTIVE _____

NOUN _____

ADJECTIVE _____

VERB ENDING IN "ING" _____

NOUN _____

VERB ENDING IN "ING" _____

NOUN _____

NOUN _____

VERB _____

NOUN _____

TYPE OF FOOD _____

PART OF THE BODY _____

MAD LIBS®

AM I IN YOUR WAY?

_____! Were you trying to type? I just felt the need to lie on
EXCLAMATION

your _____ keyboard at this moment. That _____
NOUN   NOUN

you're trying to write isn't as _____ as my nap. Oh, and did
ADJECTIVE

you want to read today's _____? Tough. It's much more
NOUN

_____ that I use it as a place to do my _____.
ADJECTIVE   VERB ENDING IN "ING"

And I hope you aren't going to do the _____ today, as I am
NOUN

planning on _____ in the laundry _____ all
VERB ENDING IN "ING"   NOUN

day, and I don't want to be disturbed. Let me know when you are

going to start preparing dinner, as I can help knock things off the

_____. And when you sit down to _____, I will
NOUN   VERB

certainly expect a few pieces of food from your _____. But
NOUN

please, no _____—you know I turn my _____ up
TYPE OF FOOD   PART OF THE BODY

at that.

MAD LIBS® is fun to play with friends, but you can also play it by yourself! To begin with, DO NOT look at the story on the page below. Fill in the blanks on this page with the words called for. Then, using the words you have selected, fill in the blank spaces in the story.

Now you've created your own hilarious MAD LIBS® game!

THE SEVEN HABITS OF HIGHLY EFFECTIVE KITTENS

PLURAL NOUN _____

ADJECTIVE _____

NOUN _____

VERB ENDING IN "ING" _____

PART OF THE BODY _____

ADJECTIVE _____

VERB _____

ADJECTIVE _____

ANIMAL _____

NOUN _____

ADJECTIVE _____

ANIMAL _____

NOUN _____

NOUN _____

NOUN _____

NOUN _____

VERB _____

MAD LIBS
THE SEVEN HABITS OF HIGHLY EFFECTIVE KITTENS

All kittens know they must perfect these _____:
PLURAL NOUN

1. Be as adorably _____ as possible at all times.
ADJECTIVE

2. Perfect that tiny, irresistible _____. Your servants will come
NOUN

_____ in a/an _____-beat.
VERB ENDING IN "ING"   _PART OF THE BODY_

3. Learn the ways of a/an _____ ninja; you can _____
ADJECTIVE   _VERB_

anywhere. It's all about stealth.

4. You must be _____, whether you're facing down
ADJECTIVE

the neighbor's _____ or jumping off the kitchen
ANIMAL

_____.
NOUN

5. You may be _____, but inside of you beats the heart of
ADJECTIVE

a/an _____. Honor your heritage.
ANIMAL

6. Make use of those _____-sharp claws. Climb the living-
NOUN

room _____ and the Christmas _____ with
NOUN   _NOUN_

courage and confidence.

7. And when you sleep, curl up in the tiniest, fluffiest _____
NOUN

possible. It will make your servants _____.
VERB

MAD LIBS® is fun to play with friends, but you can also play it by yourself! To begin with, DO NOT look at the story on the page below. Fill in the blanks on this page with the words called for. Then, using the words you have selected, fill in the blank spaces in the story.

Now you've created your own hilarious MAD LIBS® game!

YOU CALL THAT CAT FOOD?

EXCLAMATION _____

NOUN _____

ADJECTIVE _____

ANIMAL _____

ADJECTIVE _____

NOUN _____

ADJECTIVE _____

NOUN _____

ADJECTIVE _____

ADJECTIVE _____

NOUN _____

PLURAL NOUN _____

ADJECTIVE _____

NOUN _____

MAD LIBS

YOU CALL THAT CAT FOOD?

_____! What is this _____ that you put in my bowl?
  EXCLAMATION   NOUN

Do you really expect me to eat this? Have I not made it perfectly

_____ that I prefer fresh _____ to the _____
  ADJECTIVE   ANIMAL   ADJECTIVE

stuff that comes out of a/an _____? It looks _____ and
                              NOUN   ADJECTIVE

smells like a rotting _____. And I refuse to eat something that
                       NOUN

is advertised by a cat who is an embarrassment to my _____
                                         ADJECTIVE

species. Don't get so _____ when I jump onto the kitchen
                     ADJECTIVE

_____ to see what you are cooking for yourself—I might not
  NOUN

want any of that, either. Some of the _____ you make look
                             PLURAL NOUN

and smell as _____ as that _____ you try to feed me!
         ADJECTIVE   NOUN

MAD LIBS® is fun to play with friends, but you can also play it by yourself! To begin with, DO NOT look at the story on the page below. Fill in the blanks on this page with the words called for. Then, using the words you have selected, fill in the blank spaces in the story.

Now you've created your own hilarious MAD LIBS® game!

STRANGE CAT FACTS

VERB ENDING IN "ING" _____

NOUN _____

NUMBER _____

PLURAL NOUN _____

VERB _____

PLURAL NOUN _____

NUMBER _____

NUMBER _____

NOUN _____

NOUN _____

VERB _____

PART OF THE BODY _____

COLOR _____

ADJECTIVE _____

STRANGE CAT FACTS

If you think you know cats, think again:

- On average, cats spend two-thirds of every day _____.
  VERB ENDING IN "ING"

- A group of cats is called a/an " _____."
  NOUN

- A cat can jump up to _____ times its own height in a single
  NUMBER

  bound.

- Cats have over twenty _____ that control their ears.
  PLURAL NOUN

- Cats can't _____ sweetness.
  VERB

- The world's longest cat measured 48.5 _____ long.
  PLURAL NOUN

- A cat has _____ toes on its front paws, but only
  NUMBER

  _____ toes on its back paws.
  NUMBER

- When a cat leaves its _____ uncovered in the litter box, it
  NOUN

  is a/an _____ of aggression.
  NOUN

- Cats only _____ through their _____ pads.
  VERB **PART OF THE BODY**

- _____ cats are bad luck in the United States, but they are
  COLOR

  _____ luck in the United Kingdom and Australia.
  ADJECTIVE

MAD LIBS® is fun to play with friends, but you can also play it by yourself! To begin with, DO NOT look at the story on the page below. Fill in the blanks on this page with the words called for. Then, using the words you have selected, fill in the blank spaces in the story.

Now you've created your own hilarious MAD LIBS® game!

CATS IN A BOX-OR BAG

ADJECTIVE _____

VERB _____

ANIMAL (PLURAL) _____

PLURAL NOUN _____

ADJECTIVE _____

ADJECTIVE _____

ARTICLE OF CLOTHING _____

PLURAL NOUN _____

VERB _____

SAME VERB _____

ADJECTIVE _____

NOUN _____

PLURAL NOUN _____

ADJECTIVE _____

ANIMAL (PLURAL) _____

VERB _____

MAD LIBS®

CATS IN A BOX-OR BAG

Don't bother buying me some _____ toy; I won't _____
                               ADJECTIVE   VERB

with it. So skip the fake _____ filled with catnip and
                          ANIMAL (PLURAL)

those "teasers" with _____ on the ends. Just give me an old
                     PLURAL NOUN

_____ box. The secret of the old _____ box is that
ADJECTIVE   ADJECTIVE

it gives me (a/an) _____ of invisibility, enhancing my
                   ARTICLE OF CLOTHING

super-_____. When I am in the box, I can _____
      PLURAL NOUN   VERB

you, but you can't _____ me. If the box is _____,
                   SAME VERB   ADJECTIVE

that's even better, as it is more fun if I can barely get myself in it. And

it is preferable if the box has a/an _____ or _____.
                                     NOUN   PLURAL NOUN

And if you don't have a box, a/an _____ paper bag will do.
                                  ADJECTIVE

Because within the bag lives the Bag _____. And it is
                                     ANIMAL (PLURAL)

my mission in life to _____ them!
                      VERB

MAD LIBS® is fun to play with friends, but you can also play it by yourself! To begin with, DO NOT look at the story on the page below. Fill in the blanks on this page with the words called for. Then, using the words you have selected, fill in the blank spaces in the story.

Now you've created your own hilarious MAD LIBS® game!

BIG CATS

VERB _____

PLURAL NOUN _____

PLURAL NOUN _____

ADJECTIVE _____

ADJECTIVE _____

ANIMAL _____

SAME ANIMAL _____

ADJECTIVE _____

ADJECTIVE _____

VERB _____

SAME VERB _____

ADJECTIVE _____

VERB ENDING IN "ING" _____

SAME VERB ENDING IN "ING" _____

A PLACE _____

ADJECTIVE _____

NOUN _____

ADJECTIVE _____

MAD LIBS

BIG CATS

Although they don't have to _____ for their food or worry
                              VERB

about _____, domestic cats aren't all that different from their
        PLURAL NOUN

wild _____ and sisters. All cats, domestic and _____,
      PLURAL NOUN   ADJECTIVE

are _____ carnivores, whether they prefer to eat a can of
      ADJECTIVE

_____ delight or an entire raw _____. Felines
   ANIMAL   SAME ANIMAL

around the world, from _____ tabbies to _____
                         ADJECTIVE   ADJECTIVE

jaguars, _____ for sixteen to twenty hours a day. (However,
           VERB

snow leopards don't get to _____ in a basket of _____
                            SAME VERB   ADJECTIVE

laundry.) And there's the _____ thing. You might think
                          VERB ENDING IN "ING"

your cat is _____ against you because it loves you.
             SAME VERB ENDING IN "ING"

But it's marking you, just like big cats mark their territory in (the)

_____. And even though there are _____ similarities
   A PLACE   ADJECTIVE

between a house cat and a cheetah, it's much safer to have a domestic

cat in your _____—so don't get any _____ ideas!
             NOUN   ADJECTIVE

MAD LIBS® is fun to play with friends, but you can also play it by yourself! To begin with, DO NOT look at the story on the page below. Fill in the blanks on this page with the words called for. Then, using the words you have selected, fill in the blank spaces in the story.

Now you've created your own hilarious MAD LIBS® game!

CATS IN BOOKS

ADJECTIVE _____

ADJECTIVE _____

VERB ENDING IN "ING" _____

ADJECTIVE _____

PERSON IN ROOM (MALE) _____

PART OF THE BODY _____

PERSON IN ROOM (MALE) _____

A PLACE _____

ADJECTIVE _____

ADJECTIVE _____

PLURAL NOUN _____

PART OF THE BODY _____

ADJECTIVE _____

PLURAL NOUN _____

ADJECTIVE _____

PART OF THE BODY _____

MAD LIBS

CATS IN BOOKS

Test your knowledge about cats who have made their _____
ADJECTIVE

mark in literature:

- The cat who seems to be _____ and can't stop
  ADJECTIVE

  _____ at Alice: The Cheshire Cat
  VERB ENDING IN "ING"

- The _____ cat in _____ King's horror
  ADJECTIVE   PERSON IN ROOM (MALE)

  classic: Church

- The cat with a squashed _____ who belongs to
  PART OF THE BODY

  _____ Potter's best friend: Crookshanks
  PERSON IN ROOM (MALE)

- The _____ cat who is the best friend of the _____
  A PLACE   ADJECTIVE

  cockroach Archy: Mehitabel

- A mysterious, _____, and small black cat capable of
  ADJECTIVE

  performing _____ of magic and sleight of _____:
  PLURAL NOUN   PART OF THE BODY

  Mr. Mistoffelees

- The story of a very _____ kitten who struggles to keep his
  ADJECTIVE

  _____ clean and tidy: *Tom Kitten*
  PLURAL NOUN

- A/An _____ tale about a cat who wins the _____
  ADJECTIVE   PART OF THE BODY

  of a princess in marriage: *Puss in Boots*

MAD LIBS® is fun to play with friends, but you can also play it by yourself! To begin with, DO NOT look at the story on the page below. Fill in the blanks on this page with the words called for. Then, using the words you have selected, fill in the blank spaces in the story.

Now you've created your own hilarious MAD LIBS® game!

DRESSING YOUR CAT

ADJECTIVE _____

NOUN _____

PART OF THE BODY (PLURAL) _____

ANIMAL _____

ADJECTIVE _____

PERSON IN ROOM (MALE) _____

COLOR _____

PLURAL NOUN _____

OCCUPATION _____

NOUN _____

NOUN _____

ARTICLE OF CLOTHING _____

ADJECTIVE _____

NOUN _____

ADVERB _____

ADJECTIVE _____

MAD LIBS

DRESSING YOUR CAT

Your cat can help you celebrate your favorite holidays throughout

the year. All you need to do is dress it up in a/an _____,
                                                      ADJECTIVE

fun _____. With a pair of fuzzy _____,
      NOUN   PART OF THE BODY (PLURAL)

your cat can be transformed into the Easter _____. Or be
                                              ANIMAL

_____ and turn your cat into Uncle _____
 ADJECTIVE   PERSON IN ROOM (MALE)

with a little red, white, and _____ suit. And there are a lot of
                               COLOR

_____ for your cat to wear on Halloween. You can dress your
 PLURAL NOUN

cat as a/an _____ in a pink tutu, a prehistoric _____
              OCCUPATION   NOUN

with spikes down its back, or a superhero like _____-man
                                                 NOUN

with a black cape and matching _____. And of course
                                 ARTICLE OF CLOTHING

any cat can be turned into Santa Claus with a/an _____ red
                                                   ADJECTIVE

suit and a cute matching _____. Just make sure you choose
                           NOUN

_____—you don't want to get on your cat's _____
 ADVERB   ADJECTIVE

side!

MAD LIBS® is fun to play with friends, but you can also play it by yourself! To begin with, DO NOT look at the story on the page below. Fill in the blanks on this page with the words called for. Then, using the words you have selected, fill in the blank spaces in the story.

Now you've created your own hilarious MAD LIBS® game!

NINE LIVES

NOUN _____

ADJECTIVE _____

VERB ENDING IN "ING" _____

ADJECTIVE _____

ADJECTIVE _____

ANIMAL _____

ADJECTIVE _____

NOUN _____

NUMBER _____

TYPE OF LIQUID _____

NOUN _____

VERB (PAST TENSE) _____

NOUN _____

ADJECTIVE _____

VEHICLE _____

NOUN _____

NOUN _____

ADJECTIVE _____

MAD LIBS

NINE LIVES

Life #1—I ate a/an _____— a/an _____ mistake.
_{NOUN} _{ADJECTIVE}

Life #2—I didn't look both ways before _____ the street.
_{VERB ENDING IN "ING"}

_____ move.
_{ADJECTIVE}

Life #3—I was a bit too _____ when I teased the neighbor's
_{ADJECTIVE}

_____ .
_{ANIMAL}

Life #4—I thought cats were supposed to be able to survive falls from

_____ places?!
_{ADJECTIVE}

Life #5—I got locked in the _____ for _____ days
_{NOUN} _{NUMBER}

without food or _____. What's a/an _____ to do?!
_{TYPE OF LIQUID} _{NOUN}

Life #6—I _____ into the washing machine. That spin
_{VERB (PAST TENSE)}

cycle is a killer, let me tell you . . .

Life #7—I chewed through the cord to the _____. That was
_{NOUN}

a/an _____ shocker.
_{ADJECTIVE}

Life #8—I was keeping warm under the _____ when my
_{VEHICLE}

human decided to start it. I should have just taken a nap in the

_____ basket.
_{NOUN}

I have one _____ left—better make it _____!
_{NOUN} _{ADJECTIVE}